SpringerBriefs in Computer Science

Series Editors
Stan Zdonik
Peng Ning
Shashi Shekhar
Jonathan Katz
Xindong Wu
Lakhmi C. Jain
David Padua
Xuemin Shen
Borko Furht

For further volumes:
http://www.springer.com/series/10028

Xinming Ou • Anoop Singhal

Quantitative Security Risk Assessment of Enterprise Networks

 Springer

Xinming Ou
Computing and Information Sciences
Kansas State University
Manhattan, Kansas
USA
xou@ksu.edu

Anoop Singhal
Computer Security Division
National Institute of Standards
and Technology (NIST)
Gaithersburg, Maryland
USA
psinghal@nist.gov

ISSN 2191-5768   e-ISSN 2191-5776
ISBN 978-1-4614-1859-7   e-ISBN 978-1-4614-1860-3
DOI 10.1007/978-1-4614-1860-3
Springer New York Dordrecht Heidelberg London

Library of Congress Control Number: 2011941356

Printed on acid-free paper

Springer is part of Springer Science+Business Media (www.springer.com)

If you cannot measure it, you cannot improve it.
— Lord Kelvin

Preface

At present, enterprise networks constitute the core component of information technology infrastructures in areas such as power grids, financial data systems and emergency communication systems. Protection of these networks from malicious intrusions is critical to the economy and national security. To improve the security of these information systems, it is necessary to measure the amount of security provided by different networks' configurations. The objective of this book is to give an overview of the techniques and challenges for security risk analysis of computer networks. A standard model for security analysis will enable us to answer questions such as "are we more secure than yesterday or how does the security of one network configuration compare with another". Also, having a standard model to measure network security will bring together users, vendors and researchers to evaluate methodologies and products for network security.

An essential type of security risk analysis is to determine the level of compromise possible for important hosts in a network from a given starting location. This is a complex task as it depends on the network topology, security policy in the network as determined by the placement of firewalls, routers and switches and on vulnerabilities in hosts and communication protocols. Traditionally, this type of analysis is performed by a red team of computer security professionals who actively test the network by running exploits that compromise the system. Red team exercises are effective, however they are labor intensive and time consuming. There is a need for alternate approaches that can work with host vulnerability scans.

In this book, we will present a methodology for security risk analysis that is based on the model of attack graphs and the Common Vulnerability Scoring System (CVSS). Attack graphs illustrate the cumulative effect of attack steps, showing how individual steps can potentially enable an attacker to gain privileges deep within the network. CVSS is a risk measurement system that gives the likelihood that a single attack step is successfully executed. In this book we present a methodology to measure the overall system risk by combining the attack graph structure with CVSS. Our technique analyzes all attack paths through a network, providing a probabilistic metric of the overall system risk.

Acknowledgements

The authors Anoop Singhal and Ximming Ou would like to thank their colleagues who reviewed drafts of this document and contributed to its development. This material is based upon work supported by U.S. National Science Foundation under grant no. 1038366 and 1018703, AFOSR under Award No. FA9550-09-1-0138, and HP Labs Innovation Research Program. Any opinions, findings and conclusions or recommendations expressed in this material are those of the authors and do not necessarily reflect the views of the National Science Foundation, AFOSR, or Hewlett-Packard Development Company, L.P.

Contents

Acronyms

CVSS   Common Vulnerability Scoring System
NVD   National Vulnerability Database
MulVAL   Multi-host, multi-step Vulnerability Analysis Language
CERT   Computer Emergency Response Team

Chapter 1
The Need for Quantifying Security

1.1 Introduction

Enterprise networks have become essential to the operation of companies, laboratories, universities, and government agencies. As they continue to grow both in size and complexity, their security has become a critical concern. Vulnerabilities are regularly discovered in software applications which are exploited to stage cyber attacks. Currently, management of security risk of an enterprise network is more an art than a science. System administrators operate by instinct and experiences rather than relying on objective metrics to guide and justify decision making. Computer networks constitute the core component of information technology infrastructures in areas such as power grids, financial data systems and emergency communication systems. Protection of these networks from malicious intrusions is critical to the economy and security of our nation. Vulnerabilities are regularly discovered in software applications which are exploited to stage cyber attacks. Currently, management of security risk of an enterprise network is more an art than a science. System administrators operate by instinct and experience rather than relying on objective metrics to guide and justify decision making. In this book we develop models and metrics that can be used to objectively assess the security risk in an enterprise network, and techniques on how to use such metrics to guide decision making in cyber defense.

To improve the security of information systems, it is necessary to measure the amount of security provided by different network configurations. The objective of our research was to develop a standard model for measuring security of computer networks. A standard model will enable us to answer questions such as "are we more secure than yesterday or how does the security of one network configuration compare with another." Also, having a standard model to measure network security will bring together users, vendors and researchers to evaluate methodologies and products for network security. Some of the challenges for security risk analysis of enterprise networks are:

1. Security vulnerabilities are rampant: CERT reports about a hundred new security vulnerabilities each week. It becomes difficult to manage the security of an
enterprise network (with hundreds of hosts and different operating systems and
applications on each host) in the presence of software vulnerabilities that can be
exploited.
2. Attackers launch complex multi-step cyber attacks: Cyber attackers can launch
multi-step and multi-host attacks that can incrementally penetrate the network
with the goal of eventually compromising critical systems. It is a challenging
task to protect the critical systems from such attacks.
3. Current attack detection methods cannot deal with the complexity of attacks:
US computer systems are increasingly under attack. When new vulnerabilities
are reported, attack programs are available in a short amount of time. Traditional
approaches to detecting attacks (using an Intrusion Detection System) have problems such as too many false positives, limited scalability and limits on detecting.

1.2 Past Work in Security Risk Analysis

Early standardization efforts in the defense community evolved into the system
security engineering capability maturity model (SSE-CMM) [5], although it does
not assign quantitative measures. National Institute of Standards and Technology
(NIST) reports describe the security metrics implementation process [49] and principles for establishing a security baseline [48]. There are also standardization efforts
for vulnerability assessment, such as the Common Vulnerability Scoring System
(CVSS) [31], although these treat vulnerabilities in isolation, without considering
attack interdependencies on target networks. In early work in attack graph analysis, model checking was used to enumerate attack sequences linking initial and goal
states [43, 47]. Because of explicit enumeration of attack states, these approaches
scale exponentially with the size of the network. With a practical assumption of
monotonic logic, attack graph complexity has been shown to be polynomial rather
than exponential [7, 25]. Graph complexity has been further reduced, to worst-case
quadratic in the number of hosts [33]. Further improvement is possible by grouping
networks into protection domains, in which there is unrestricted connectivity among
hosts within each domain [35]. With this representation, complexity is reduced to
linear within each protection domain, and overall quadratic in the number of protection domains (which is typically much less than the number of hosts). Such attack
graphs have been generated for tens of thousands of hosts (hundreds of domains)
within a minute, excluding graph visualization. Beyond improving attack graph
complexity, frameworks have been proposed for expressing network attack models [34, 11, 51]. Capabilities for mapping multi-step attacks have begun to appear
in some commercial products [4, 2], although their limitations include not showing
all possible attack paths simultaneously as needed for effective risk assessment. A
more extensive review of attack graph research (as of 2005) is given in [26].

The issue of security metrics has long attracted much attention [23, 29, 30], and recent years have seen significant effort on the development of quantitative security metrics [6, 9, 10, 28, 32, 40, 45]. However, difficulty remains on how to establish metrics that can objectively quantify security risk in an enterprise network. Such risks are implied not only by the number of vulnerabilities, but also by the structure of security interactions among the hosts and services in an enterprise network. Attack graph is a natural candidate for representing this structure, providing an opportunity to start building a metric model for the security risks. Recently works have emerged that utilize attack graph structures and individual vulnerability metrics (such as CVSS [31]) to compute cumulative risk metrics for enterprise networks [8, 14, 15, 17, 54, 56, 57, 58]. Frigault et. al [14] propose converting attack graphs and individual vulnerability score into Bayesian Network for computing the cumulative probability. Wang et al [54] recognize the existence of cycles in an attack graph and present ideas about how to propagate probabilities over cycles. In [28] the concept of "Attack Surface" is used to determine the security risk of software systems.

Good metrics should be measured consistently, are inexpensive to collect, are expressed numerically, have units of measure, and have specific context [21]. We meet this challenge by capturing vulnerability interdependencies and measuring security in the exact way that real attackers penetrate the network. We analyze all attack paths through a network, providing a metric of overall system risk. Through this metric, we analyze tradeoffs between security costs and security benefits. Decision makers can therefore avoid over investing in security measures that do not pay off, or under investing and risking devastating consequences. Our metric is consistent, unambiguous, and provides context for understanding security risk of computer networks. Security metrics have been suggested based on criteria compliance, intrusion detection, security policy, security incidents, and actuarial modeling. Statistical methods (Markov modeling, Bayesian networks, etc.) have been used in measuring network security. Complementary to our approach, measurements of attack resistance [53] and weakest successful adversary [40] have been proposed.

In this book we identify two layers in enterprise network security metrics: the component metrics and the cumulative metrics. The component metrics are about individual components properties which in many cases can be obtained from standard data sources like the National Vulnerability Database (NVD). The important feature of the component metrics is that they are only about individual components and do not consider interactions among components. As a result they can be measured or computed separately. The cumulative security metrics account for both the baseline metrics of individual components and the interactions among components. We propose that the cumulative metrics shall be obtained by composing the component metrics through a sound theoretical model with well-defined semantics.

Chapter 2
Attack Graph Techniques

2.1 An example scenario

Modern attack-graph techniques can automatically discover *all* possible ways an attacker can compromise an enterprise network by analyzing configuration information of the hosts and network [7, 12, 13, 19, 20, 24, 26, 27, 37, 38, 39, 41, 44, 46, 47, 50, 52]. We will use the MulVAL logical attack graph [38, 39] as the foundation to build the metric models. A logical attack graph directly encodes the logical causality relationship among configuration settings and potential attacker privileges. It shows "why an attack can happen", instead of "how an attack happens" as in some earlier attack-graph works [41, 46, 47, 50]. Its semantics is similar to the "exploit dependency attack graph" in the Cauldron project [7, 20, 35], and to a lesser degree also similar to the "multiple-prerequisite attack graph" [19] in the NetSPA project [27]. Thus our methodology could also be applied in combination with the other attack graph models. The advantage of MulVAL is that the logical relationship is clear and explicit in the attack graph representation and the graph generation is scalable. The asymptotic complexity of MulVAL attack graph generation is $O(n^2)$ where n is the number of machines in the network, and it can generate attack graphs with a thousand machines in minutes [38]. Recently Saha shows that by generating MulVAL logical attack graphs directly in the XSB [42] logic engine the graph generation time can be further reduced [44].

The semantics of MulVAL attack graphs is best explained with an example. In the small enterprise network shown in Figure 2.1, there are three subnets mediated by an external and an internal firewall. The web server is in the DMZ subnet and is directly accessible from the Internet through the external firewall. The database server is located in the Internal subnet and holds sensitive information. It is only accessible from the web server and the User subnet. The User subnet contains the user workstations used by the company's employees. The firewalls allow all out-bound traffic from the User subnet. The web server contains the vulnerability CVE-2006-

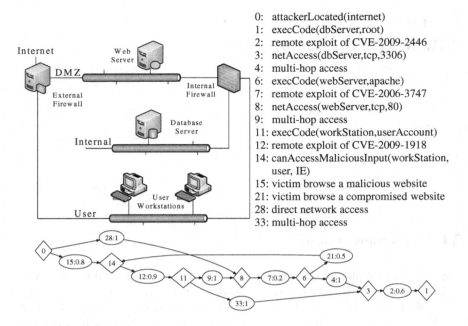

0: attackerLocated(internet)
1: execCode(dbServer,root)
2: remote exploit of CVE-2009-2446
3: netAccess(dbServer,tcp,3306)
4: multi-hop access
6: execCode(webServer,apache)
7: remote exploit of CVE-2006-3747
8: netAccess(webServer,tcp,80)
9: multi-hop access
11: execCode(workStation,userAccount)
12: remote exploit of CVE-2009-1918
14: canAccessMaliciousInput(workStation, user, IE)
15: victim browse a malicious website
21: victim browse a compromised website
28: direct network access
33: multi-hop access

Fig. 2.1 Example scenario and attack graph

3747^1 in the Apache HTTP service which can result in a remote attacker possibly executing arbitrary code on the machine. The database server contains the vulnerability CVE-2009-2446 in the MySQL database service which could allow administrator access. The user workstations contain the vulnerability CVE-2009-1918 in the Internet Explorer. If a user accesses malicious content using the vulnerable IE browser the machine may be compromised. After analyzing the configuration of this network, MulVAL outputs an attack graph shown below the network diagram. The labels of the graph nodes are displayed at the righthand side of the network diagram.

There are two types of vertices in the attack graph[2]. The diamond vertices represent privileges an attacker could obtain through exploiting the vulnerabilities in the system. An elliptic vertex represents an attack step that can lead to a privilege. Node 0 is the attacker's initial privilege which in this case is a vantage point at the Internet. An attack can only be accomplished when all its pre-conditions are met; thus the incoming arcs to an attack-step vertex form a logical AND relation. For example, node 7 (shown as "7:0.2" in the graph) represents the exploit of the web server vulnerability and the exploit can only happen when the attacker can access tcp port 80 on the web server (node 8). Multiple incoming arcs to a privilege vertex indicates

---

[1] Common Vulnerabilities and Exposures (CVE) is a dictionary of common names (i.e., CVE Identifiers) for publicly known information security vulnerabilities http://cve.mitre.org/

[2] MulVAL attack graph also has a third type of vertices which are facts about system configuration. They are omitted for presentation clarity.

more than one way to obtain the privilege and thus form a logical OR relation. For example, privilege 3 (network access to the MySQL service on the database server) can be obtained either through compromising the web server (6) or the workstation (11).

A careful examination of the attack graph reveals a number of intrusion paths leading to the compromise of the various hosts. An attacker could first compromise the web server and use it as a stepping stone to further attack the database server (0, 28, 8, 7, 6, 4, 3, 2, 1). Or he could first gain control on a user workstation by tricking a user to click a malicious link, and launch further attacks from the workstation (0,15,14, 12, 11, ...). There are many other attack paths. In general if we enumerate all possible attack paths in a system the number will be exponential. However, the privileges and attacks on all these paths are inter-dependent on each other and the number of pair-wise inter-dependencies is quadratic to the size of the network. Instead of enumerating all attack paths, a logical attack graph like MulVAL enumerates the inter-dependencies among the attacks and privileges. This provides an efficient polynomial-time algorithm for computing a compact representation of *all* attack paths in a system.

Although the example attack graph is computed from known vulnerabilities, attack graphs are equally powerful in reasoning about unknown (zero-day) vulnerabilities [18, 39], by introducing hypothetical vulnerabilities in the input. Such hypothetical vulnerabilities can be marked in the produced attack graphs and handled accordingly in the subsequent analysis.

Attack graphs are often perceived to offer a deterministic view of enterprise network security: an attack can succeed as long as all its preconditions are met, and a privilege can be obtained as long as the graph shows a path leading to it from the attacker's initial privilege. This type of deterministic semantics is certainly valuable and one can use it to conduct various types of useful analysis [13, 16, 22, 25, 27, 36, 44, 55]. However, the reality of practical enterprise security management is far from a clear-cut zero/one view. Take the vulnerability CVE-2006-3747 on the web server as an example. The official description found on the CVE website (http://cve.mitre.org/cgi-bin/cvename.cgi?name=CVE-2006-3747) says:

> Off-by-one error in the ldap scheme handling in the Rewrite module (mod_rewrite) in Apache 1.3 from 1.3.28, 2.0.46 and other versions before 2.0.59, and 2.2, when RewriteEngine is enabled, allows remote attackers to cause a denial of service (application crash) and possibly execute arbitrary code via crafted URLs that are not properly handled using certain rewrite rules.

The word "possibly" highlights that the true consequence of exploiting the vulnerability is far from certain. Since this vulnerability is one of the first stepping stones for the subsequent attacks, the likelihood for an attacker to obtain the other privileges are also affected by the likelihood he can succeed at this first stage. A system administrator would typically conduct some research on the web to "get a sense" on how likely an attacker, given access to the vulnerability, would be able to successfully exploit it. He then combines this with the specific situation in his own network to gauge the risk. This is an important process since most organizations operate under limited resources and cannot afford to fix all potential security problems. Without an understanding of the likelihood a vulnerability can lead to real damage, it will be hard to see how the potential damage compares to the costs incurred by the various countermeasures (*e.g.* down time due to patching) and make sensible decisions. Unfortunately there is currently no quantitative models that can help administrators make such decisions, and as a result security management of enterprise networks is still a "black art". Our proposed research attempts to transform this field into a science by designing objective quantitative security metrics built upon attack-graph techniques. Logical relations encoded in attack graphs are highly important in gauging security risks, but one must go beyond the deterministic view and admit the inherent uncertainty in risk assessment.

2.2 Tools for Generating Attack Graphs

- TVA (Topological Analysis of Network Attack Vulnerability) In [33, 35, 20] the authors describe a tool for generation of attack graphs. This approach assumes the monotonicity property of attacks and it has polynomial time complexity. The central idea is to use an exploit dependency graph to represent the pre and post conditions for an exploit. Then a graph search algorithm is used to chain the individual vulnerabilities and find attack paths that involve multiple vulnerabilities.
- NETSPA (A Network Security Planning Architecture) In [19, 18] the authors use attack graphs to model adversaries and the effect of simple counter measures. It creates a network model using firewall rules and network vulnerability scans. It then uses the model to compute network reachability and attack graphs representing potential attack paths for adversaries exploiting known vulnerabilities. This discovers all hosts that can be compromised by an attacker starting from one or more locations. NETSPA typically scales as $O(nlogn)$ as the number of hosts in a typical network increases. Risk is assessed for different adversaries by measuring the total assets that can be captured by an attacker.
- MULVAL (Multihost, multistage, Vulnerability Analysis) In [38, 39] a network security analyzer based on Datalog is described. The information in vulnerability databases, the configuration information for each machine and other relevant information are all encoded as Datalog facts. The reasoning engine captures the interaction among various components in the network. The reasoning engine in MULVAL scales well ($O(n^2)$) with the size of the network.

Skybox security [4] and Red Seal Systems [2] have developed a tool that can generate attack graphs. Risk is calculated using the probability of success of an attack path multiplied by the loss associated with the compromised target. Nessus [1] and Retina [3] are vulnerability management systems that can help organizations with vulnerability assessment, mitigation and protection.

Chapter 3
The Common Vulnerability Scoring System (CVSS)

CVSS is an industry standard for assessing the severity of computer system security vulnerabilities. It attempts to establish a measure of how much concern a vulnerability warrants, compared to other vulnerabilities, so efforts can be prioritized. It offers the following benefits:

- Standardized Vulnerability Scores: When an organization normalizes vulnerability scores across all of its software and hardware platforms, it can leverage a single vulnerability management policy.
- Open Framework: Users can be confused when a vulnerability is assigned an arbitrary score. With CVSS, anyone can see the individual characteristics used to derive a score.
- Prioritized Risk: When the environmental score is computed, the vulnerability now becomes contextual. That is, vulnerability scores are now representative of the actual risk to an organization.

CVSS is composed of three metric groups: Base, Temporal, and Environmental, each consisting of a set of metrics, as shown in Figure 2.

Fig. 3.1 CVSS Metric Groups

These metric groups are described as follows:

- Base: representing "intrinsic and fundamental characteristics of a vulnerability that are constant over time and user environments"

- Temporal: representing "characteristics of a vulnerability that change over time but not among user environments"
- Environmental: representing "characteristics of a vulnerability that are relevant and unique to a particular user's environment"

The base metric group captures the characteristics of a vulnerability that do not change with time and across user environment. The Access Vector, Access Complexity, and Authentication metrics capture how the vulnerability is accessed and whether or not extra conditions are required to exploit it. The three impact metrics measure how a vulnerability, if exploited, will directly effect the degree of loss of confidentiality, integrity, and availability. For example, a vulnerability could cause a partial loss of integrity and availability, but no loss of confidentiality. We briefly describe the metrics as follows.

Access Vector (AV): This metric reflects how the vulnerability is exploited. The possible values for this metrics are: Local (L), Adjacent Network (A), and Network (N). The more remote an attacker can attack a host, the greater the vulnerability score.

Access Complexity (AC): This metric measures the complexity of the attack required to exploit the vulnerability once an attacker has gained access to the target system. The possible values for this metrics are: High (H), Medium (M), Low (L). For example, consider a buffer overflow in an Internet service. Once the target system is located, the attacker can launch and exploit it at will. The lower the required complexity, the higher the vulnerability score.

Authentication (AU) This metric measures the number of times an attacker must authenticate in order to exploit a vulnerability. This metric does not gauge the strength complexity of authentication process, but only that an attacker is required to provide credentials before an exploit is launched. The possible values for this metric are: Multiple (M), Single (S), None (N). The fewer authentication instances that are required, the higher the vulnerability scores.

Confidentiality Impact (C): This metric measures the impact on confidentiality of a successfully exploited vulnerability. Confidentiality refers to limiting information access and disclosure to only authorized users, as well as preventing access by, or disclosure to, unauthorized ones. The possible values for this metric are: None (N), Partial (P), Complete (C). Increased confidentiality impact increases the vulnerability score.

Integrity Impact (I): This metric measures the impact to integrity of a successfully exploited vulnerability. Integrity refers to the trustworthiness and guaranteed veracity of information. The possible values for this metric are: None (N), Partial (P), Complete (C). Increased integrity impact increases the vulnerability score.

Availability Impact (A): This metric measures the impact to availability caused by a successfully exploited vulnerability. Availability refers to the accessibility of information resources. Attacks that consume network bandwidth, processor cycles, or disk space all impact the availability of a system. The possible values for this metric are: None (N), Partial (P), Complete (C). Increased availability impact increases the vulnerability score.

3.1 An Example

Consider CVE-2003-0062: Buffer Overflow in NOD32 Antivirus. NOD32 is an antivirus software application developed by Eset. In February 2003, a buffer overflow vulnerability was discovered in Linux and Unix versions prior to 1.013 that could allow local users to execute arbitrary code with the privileges of the user executing NOD32. To trigger the buffer overflow, the attacker must wait for (or coax) another user (possible root) to scan a directory path of excessive length.

Since the vulnerability is exploitable only to a user locally logged into the system, the Access Vector is Local. The Access Complexity is High because this vulnerability can be exploited only under specialized access conditions. There is an additional layer of complexity because the attacker must wait for another user to run the virus scanning software. Authentication is set to None because the attacker does not need to authenticate to any additional system. Together, these metrics produce a base score of 6.2.

The base vector for this vulnerability is :AV:L/AC:H/Au:N/C:C/I:C/A:C

Base Metric	Evaluation	Score
Access Vector	[Local]	(0.395)
Access Complexity	[High]	(0.35)
Authentication	[None]	(0.704)
Confidentiality Impact	[Complete]	(0.66)
Integrity Impact	[Complete]	(0.66)
Availability Impact	[Complete]	(0.66)

$$
\begin{aligned}
Impact &= 10.41 * (1(0.34 * 0.34 * 0.34)) == 10.0 \\
Exploitability &= 20 * 0.35 * 0.704 * 0.395 == 1.9 \\
f(Impact) &= 1.176 \\
BaseScore &= ((0.6 * 10) + (0.4 * 1.9) - 1.5) * 1.176 = 6.2
\end{aligned}
$$

Table 3.1 Example CVSS metrics

Basically, for each metric group, an equation is used to weigh the corresponding metrics and produce a score (ranged from 0 to 10) based on a series of measurements and security experts assessment, and the score 10 represents the most severe vulnerability. Specifically, when the base metrics are assigned values, the base equation calculates a score ranging from 0 to 10, and creates a vector. This vector is a text string that contains the values assigned to each metric. It is used to communicate exactly how the score for each vulnerability is derived, so that anyone can understand how the score was derived and, if desired, confirm the validity of each metric.

Optionally, the base score can be refined by assigning values to the temporal and environmental metrics. This is useful in order to provide additional context for a vulnerability by more accurately reflecting the risk posed by the vulnerability to a users environment. Depending on ones purpose, the base score and vector may be sufficient. If a temporal score is needed, the temporal equation will combine the temporal metrics with the base score to produce a temporal score ranging from 0 to 10. Similarly, if an environmental score is needed, the environmental equation will combine the environmental metrics with the base score to produce an environmental score ranging from 0 to 10. More details on base, temporal and environmental equations, and the calculations can be found in the CVSS standards guide [31]

Chapter 4
Security Risk Analysis of Enterprise Networks Using Attack Graphs

In this chapter we present our methodology of security risk analysis of Enterprise Networks using Attack Graphs. We explain our methodology using three examples. Attack graphs provide the cumulative effect of attack steps to show how each of these steps can potentially enable an attacker to reach his goal. However, one limitation of attack graph is that it assumes that a vulnerability can always be exploited. In reality, there is a wide range of probabilities that different steps can be exploited. It is dependent on the skill of the attacker and the difficulty of the exploit. Attack graphs show what is possible without any indication of what is likely. In this section, we present a methodology to estimate the security risk using the scores of individual vulnerabilities.

4.1 Example 1

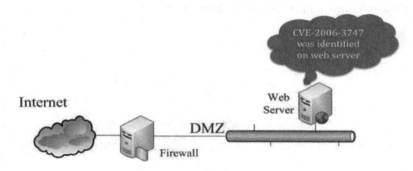

Fig. 4.1 Example 1

In the simple example of Figure 4.2, there is a firewall controlling network access from Internet to the DMZ subnet of an enterprise network. The Demilitarized Zone

(DMZ) is typically used to place publicly accessible servers, in this case the web server. The firewall protects the host in DMZ and only allows external access to ports necessary for the service. In this example, Internet is allowed to access the web server through TCP port 80, the standard HTTP protocol and port.

Suppose a vulnerability scan is performed on the web server, and a vulnerability is identified. The CVE ID of the discovered vulnerability is CVE-2006-3747. Using this ID as a key, one can query the National Vulnerability Database (NVD) and obtain a number of important properties of the vulnerability. Below is an excerpt from the information retrieved from NVD about CVE-2006-3747:

Overview

Off-by-one error in the ldap scheme handling in the Rewrite module (mod_rewrite) in Apache 1.3 from 1.3.28, 2.0.46 and other versions before 2.0.59, and 2.2, when RewriteEngine is enabled, allows remote attackers to cause a denial of service (application crash) and possibly execute arbitrary code via crafted URLs that are not properly handled using certain rewrite rules.

Impact

CVSS Severity (version 2.0): CVSS v2 Base Score:7.6 (HIGH) (AV:N/AC:H/Au:N/C:C/I:C/A:C) (legend) Impact Subscore: 10.0 Exploitability Subscore: 4.9 CVSS Version 2 Metrics: Access Vector: Network exploitable Access Complexity: High Authentication: Not required to exploit Impact Type: Provides administrator access, Allows complete confidentiality, integrity, and availability violation; Allows unauthorized disclosure of information; Allows disruption of service

The "Overview" section gives a number of key features of the vulnerability, including the relevant software modules and versions and what security impact the vulnerability poses to a system. The latter is further displayed in the "Impact" section. Most of the impact factors are expressed in the CVSS metric vector, which is "AV:N/AC:H/Au:N/C:C/I:C/A:C" in this case.

These CVSS metrics provide crucial information regarding the pre- and post-conditions for exploiting the vulnerability. Such information can then be used to construct an attack graph which shows all possible attack paths in a network. The attack graph for this simple network is shown in Figure 4.

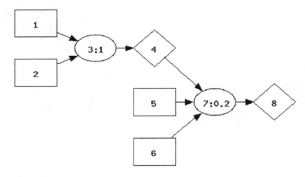

Fig. 4.2 Attack Graph for Example 1

The meaning of the node labels are explained below:

1. hacl(internet,webServer,httpProtocol,httpPort)
2. attackerLocated(internet)
3. direct network access
4. netAccess(webServer,httpProtocol,httpPort)
5. networkServiceInfo(webServer,httpd,httpProtocol,httpPort,apache)
6. vulExists(webServer,'CVE-2006-3747',httpd,remote,privEscalation)
7. remote exploit of a server program
8. execCode(webServer,apache)

The above graph is computed from the MulVAL network security analyzer [31, 32]. The square vertices represent configuration of the system, e.g., the existence of a software vulnerability on a machine (node 6), firewall rules that allow Internet to access the web server through the HTTP protocol and port (node 1), and services running on a host (node 5). The diamond vertices represent potential privileges an attacker could gain in the system, e.g., code execution privilege on web server (node 8). The elliptical vertices are attack nodes which links preconditions to post-conditions of an attack. For example, node 7 represents the attack remote exploit of a server program. Its preconditions are: the attacker has network access to the target machine for the specific protocol and port (node 4), the service on that port is running (node 5), and the service is vulnerable (node 6). The post-condition of the attack is that the attacker gains the specific privilege on the machine (node 8).

An attack graph can help a system administrator understand what could happen in his network, through analyzing the configuration of an enterprise network system. When the size of the system increases, it becomes increasingly difficult for a human to keep track of and correlate all relevant information. An automatic attack-graph generator has its unique advantage in that it can identify non-obvious attack possibilities arising from intricate security interactions within an enterprise network, which can be easily missed by a human analyst. It achieves this through building up a knowledge base (KB) about generic security knowledge independent of any specific scenarios. For example, the KB rule that generated part of the attack graph in Figure 4 is shown below.

```
execCode(H, Perm)  :-
    vulExists(H, VulID, Software, remote, privEscalation),
    networkServiceInfo(H, Software, Protocol, Port, Perm),
    netAccess(H, Protocol, Port).
```

This is a generic Datalog rule for how to reason about remote exploit of a service program. It is easy to see that the three subgoals correspond to the three predecessors of node 7, and the head of the rule corresponds to its successor. The variables (in upper case-led identifiers) are automatically instantiated with the concrete values from a systems configuration tuples. There are many other rules like the one above in the KB. All the rules form a Datalog program and a Prolog system can efficiently evaluate such a program against thousands of input tuples. The evaluation process is guaranteed to find out all consequences arising from the rules on the input facts through arbitrary number of steps of derivation. Complex multi-step, multi-host attack paths are naturally captured in this logical reasoning process, even though each rule itself only describes a specific type of attacks.

An attack graph is often perceived to have a deterministic semantics: as long as all the pre-conditions of an attack can be achieved, the attack can always succeed resulting in the attacker obtaining the post-condition privilege. In reality, it is often not that clearly-cut black and white. The possibly execute arbitrary code in the vulnerabilitys overview highlights the uncertainty in the true consequence of exploiting a vulnerability. Depending on the difficulty level of the exploit, the attackers skills and resources, and how hard it is to get to it, a vulnerability may or may not pose a high risk to the system. Since all security hardening measures (e.g. patching) inevitably incurs cost in terms of human labor, increased inconvenience, or degraded performance, security administration is an art of balancing risk and cost. A quantitative model for risk assessment is indispensable to make this effort a more scientific process.

Deriving security metrics from attack graphs.

Since all the attack nodes in an attack graph do not always guarantee success, we can attach a component metric to each attack node. The component metric is a numeric measure indicating the conditional probability of attack success when all the preconditions are met. Such component metrics can be derived from CVSS metric vector. For example, we can map the AC metric to probability such that higher AC metric value is mapped to a lower value in probability. Then we can aggregate the probabilities over the attack-graph structure to provide a cumulative metric, which indicates the absolute probability of attack success in the specific system. The cumulative metrics are not only affected by the individual vulnerabilities properties, but is also to a large extend affected by how the security interactions may happen in the specific system which affects the way an attacker can move from one step to another. By combining the component metrics with the attack-graph structure, one can obtain a security metric that is tailored to the specific environment, instead of a generic metric such as the CVSS Base Score.

In the example attack graph of Figure 4, node 7 is attached a component metric 0.2 which is derived from the vulnerabilitys AC metric based on the mapping High $\rightarrow$ 0.2, Medium $\rightarrow$ 0.6, Low $\rightarrow$ 0.9. Node 3 has a component metric 1 since it represents network access semantics, not a real attack step and thus without an uncertainty in its success. Since this attack graph is very simple, we can easily see that the cumulative metric for node 8 (compromise of the web server) is also 0.2.

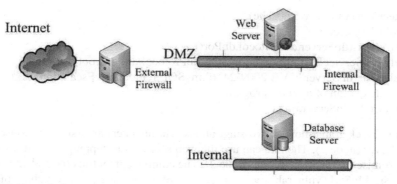

Fig. 4.3 Example 2

4.2 Example 2

In this example a new subnet Internal is added, which hosts the database server. The access to the Internal subnet is mediated by an internal firewall. Only the web server can access the database server, which also has a remote vulnerability in the MySQL DB service (CVE-2009-2446). The attack graph for this network is shown in Figure 4.4.

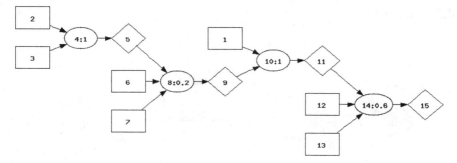

Fig. 4.4 Example 2 Attack Graph

1. hacl(webServer,dbServer,dbProtocol,dbPort)
2. hacl(internet,webServer,httpProtocol,httpPort)
3. attackerLocated(internet)
4. direct network access
5. netAccess(webServer,httpProtocol,httpPort)
6. networkServiceInfo(webServer,httpd,httpProtocol,httpPort,apache)
7. vulExists(webServer,'CVE-2006-3747',httpd,remote,privEscalation)
8. remote exploit of a server program

9. execCode(webServer,apache)
10. multi-hop access
11. netAccess(dbServer,dbProtocol,dbPort)
12. networkServiceInfo(dbServer,mySQL,dbProtocol,dbPort,root)
13. vulExists(dbServer,'CVE-2009-2446',mySQL,remote,privEscalation)
14. remote exploit of a server program
15. execCode(dbServer,root)

This attack graph shows a two-stage attack. The attacker can first compromise the web server (node 7). Then he can use the web server as a stepping stone to further compromise the database server (node 2). The component metrics for node 2 is 0.6, since the MySQL vulnerability is easier to exploit than the Apache vulnerability. In this attack graph, since there is only one path to reach the compromise of the database sever (node 1), it is easy to see that the cumulative metric for node 1 is the multiplication of the two component metrics on the path: 0.2x0.6=0.12. This is intuitive since the longer the attack path, the lower the risk.

This example highlights the need to account for security interactions in the specific network to fully understand the risk a vulnerability brings to a system. Although the vulnerability on the database server has a high CVSS score (8.5 in this case), the cumulative risk contributed by the vulnerability to the specific system may be marginal, since it is located at a placed hard to get to by an attacker.

4.3 Example 3

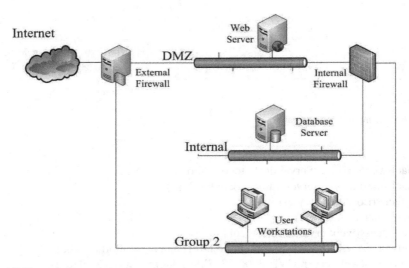

Fig. 4.5 Example 3

Example three adds another subnet to the network, called Group 2. This subnet contains the user desktop machines used by the companys employees. These machines run the Windows operating system and Internet Explorer (IE) browser. Vulnerability CVE-2009-1918 was identified in IE that would enable execution of arbitrary code on the victims machine. To exploit this vulnerability, an attacker must trick a user into visiting a maliciously-crafted web page. The vulnerability is not a highly complex one to exploit, i.e. once a user falls in the trap, it is highly likely his/her machine will be compromised. The other two vulnerabilities discussed above also exist on the web server and database server in this example. The attack graph for this network is shown in Figure 4.6.

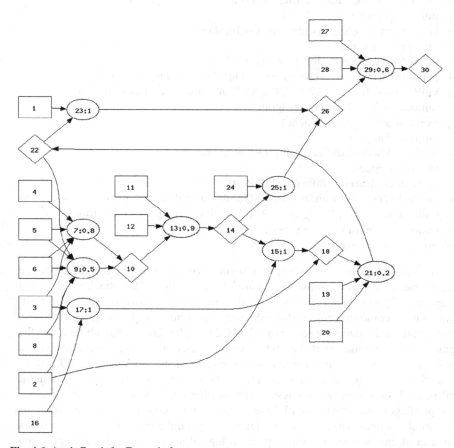

Fig. 4.6 Attak Graph for Example 3

1. hacl(webServer,dbServer,dbProtocol,dbPort)
2. hacl(workStation,webServer,httpProtocol,httpPort)
3. attackerLocated(internet)

 4. hacl(workStation,internet,httpProtocol,httpPort)
 5. isClient('IE')
 6. inCompetent(secretary)
 7. Browsing a malicious website
 8. isWebServer(webServer)
 9. Browsing a compromised website
10. accessMaliciousInput(workStation,secretary,'IE')
11. hasAccount(secretary,workStation,normalAccount)
12. vulExists(workStation,'CVE-2009-1918','IE',remote,privEscalation)
13. remote exploit of a client program
14. execCode(workStation,normalAccount)
15. multi-hop access
16. hacl(internet,webServer,httpProtocol,httpPort)
17. direct network access
18. netAccess(webServer,httpProtocol,httpPort)
19. networkServiceInfo(webServer,httpd,httpProtocol,httpPort,apache)
20. vulExists(webServer,'CVE-2006-3747',httpd,remote,privEscalation)
21. remote exploit of a server program
22. execCode(webServer,apache)
23. multi-hop access
24. hacl(workStation,dbServer,dbProtocol,dbPort)
25. multi-hop access
26. netAccess(dbServer,dbProtocol,dbPort)
27. networkServiceInfo(dbServer,mySQL,dbProtocol,dbPort,root)
28. vulExists(dbServer,'CVE-2009-2446',mySQL,remote,privEscalation)
29. remote exploit of a server program
30. execCode(dbServer,root)

In even such a small network, how security on one machine can affect another can be manifold and non-obvious. A careful examination of the attack graph reveals a number of potential intrusion paths leading to the compromise of the various hosts. An attacker could first compromise the web server and use it as a stepping stone to further attack the database server (3, 17, 18, 21, 22, 23, 26, 29, 30). Or he could first gain control on a user workstation by tricking a user into clicking a malicious link, and launch attacks against the database server from the workstation (3, 7, 10, 13, 14, 25, 26, 29, 30). There are many other attack paths. In general if we enumerate all possible attack paths in a system the number could be exponential. However, the privileges and attacks on all these paths are inter-dependent on each other and the number of pair-wise inter-dependencies is quadratic to the size of the network. Instead of enumerating all attack paths, a logical attack graph like MulVAL enumerates the inter-dependencies among the attacks and privileges. This provides an efficient polynomial-time algorithm for computing a compact representation of all attack paths in a system.

There are a number of attack nodes in this graph. Node 21 and 29 are the exploit against the web server and database server respectively, which have been explained before. An interesting node is 13 which is about the exploit of the IE vulnerability. The component metric 0.9 indicates that this exploit has a high success rate when all the preconditions are met. Of the three preconditions, one of them is that the user (secretary) must access malicious input through the IE program on the host (node 10). This precondition is further calculated by two rules. Node 7 is the instantiation of the following rule:

```
accessMaliciousInput(H, Victim, Software) :-
    inCompetent(Victim),
    isClient(Software),
    hacl(H, MaliciousMachine, httpProtocol, httpPort),
    attackerLocated(MaliciousMachine).
```

The predicate "inCompetent" indicates that somebody is not trustworthy for using computers carefully and may fall victim of social-engineering attacks, e.g. clicking a malicious url. The predicate isClient indicates that a piece of software is a client software and as a result the exploit of the vulnerability will need user assistance. This type of information can be obtained from the NVD data as well. Intuitively, the clause specifies that if someone is not careful, and his machine can access a malicious host controlled by an attacker, he may access malicious input provided by the attacker. The component metric assigned to this likelihood is 0.8 as shown in the graph. Basically this number will need to be provided by the user of the risk analysis tool. Node 9 captures another scenario for the user to access malicious input: he may browse to a compromised web site. This could happen in this network since the attacker could compromise the corporate web server (node 22) and the firewall allows the user workstation to access the corporate web server (node 2). The component metric for node 9 is 0.5, again input by the users. The component metrics like those for node 7 and 9 are different from those associated with vulnerabilities. They are affected by the security awareness of users of the enterprise system and is thus context-specific. To provide these metric values, the risk analysis tool can conduct an initial survey asking multiple-choice questions like how likely will the user of workstations visit a malicious web site? Based on the answers provided by the system administrator, a set of component metrics representing the above likelihood can be derived and used in subsequent analyses.

It is less obvious how to calculate in this attack graph the likelihood an attacker can obtain a privilege (e.g. node 30, code-execution privilege on the database server). The complexity comes from shared dependencies and cycles that exist in this attack graph. A number of methods have been developed to handle such complexities and to calculate attack success likelihood in arbitrary attack graphs [25, 34]. We will use this example to illustrate how to use such calculated metrics to aid in security administration.

4.4 Using risk metrics to prioritize security hardening

When considering improvements in network security, a network administrator is constrained in terms of money and time. For example, some changes, though preferable, may not be feasible because of the time necessary to make the change and the system downtime that would occur while the change was made. Considering the network topology in example 3, it is not immediately clear which of the vulnerabilities should be patched first, assuming that a fix is available for each of the three.

Host	Initial scenario	Patch web server	Patch db server	Patch workstations	Change network access
Database server	0.47	0.43	0	0.12	0.12
Web server	0.2	0	0.2	0.2	0.2
Workstations	0.74	0.72	0.74	0	0.74

Table 4.1 Probabilities of compromise for hosts in Figure 2.1 (columns reflect different scenarios)

Table 4.1 shows the metric calculation results based on the method of Homer et al. [34]. Column 2 shows the risk metrics for example 3. Column 3-6 show the new risk assessment values based on various mitigation options: patching different vulnerabilities or changing the firewall rules so that the user workstations cannot access the database server.

Patching the vulnerability on the web server would eliminate the known risk of compromise for the web server, but have little effect on the other two hosts. The web server does not contain sensitive information, so protecting this host first may not be the best choice.

Patching the vulnerability on the database server would eliminate the known risk of compromise for the database server, but have no effect on the risk in the other two hosts, since privileges on the database server do not enable new attacks on the other hosts. This option would secure the sensitive data on the database server, which may be most desirable, but at the cost of having a period of downtime on the database server which may affect business revenues.

Patching the vulnerability on the user workstations would eliminate the risk on itself, as well as significantly reducing the risk in the database server, though the risk in the web server is unchanged. This option secures the workstations and makes the database server more secure, which may be a better solution.

Network configuration changes can also have drastic effects on the security risk. The final column in the table shows the effect of blocking network access from the workstations to the database server. This option eliminates an attack path to the database server that depends on privileges on the workstations, lowering the risk of compromise for the database server, but leaving the web server and workstations vulnerable. Depending on other resource constraints and asset valuations, this may also be a viable solution. There may not be a single "best" option for all organizations. Indeed, different administrators could easily make different choices in this same situation, based on the perceived importance of the hosts and the expected time necessary to carry out a mediation, as well as human resources available. The quantitative risk metrics make clear the effects emerging from each of these possible changes, providing a network administrator with objective data beneficial for judging the relative value of each option.

Chapter 5
Conclusion

We have presented an approach to aggregating vulnerability metrics in an enterprise network through attack graphs. Our approach is sound in that, given component metrics which characterize the likelihood that individual vulnerabilities can be successfully exploited, the model computes a numeric value representing the cumulative likelihood for an attacker to succeed in gaining a specific privilege or carrying out an attack in the network. This method can be used to help system administrators decide between risk mitigation options.

References

1. Nessus vulnerability scanner. http://www.nessus.org.
2. Redseal systems. http://www.redseal.net/.
3. Retina security scanner. http://www.eeye.com/.
4. Skybox security. http://www.skyboxsecurity.com/.
5. The systems security engineering capability maturity model.   http://www.sse-cmm.org/index.html.
6. Ehab Al-Shaer, Latif Khan, and M. Salim Ahmed. A comprehensive objective network security metric framework for proactive security configuration. In *ACM Cyber Security and Information Intelligence Research Workshop*, 2008.
7. Paul Ammann, Duminda Wijesekera, and Saket Kaushik. Scalable, graph-based network vulnerability analysis. In *Proceedings of 9th ACM Conference on Computer and Communications Security*, Washington, DC, November 2002.
8. Zahid Anwar, Ravinder Shankesi, and Roy H. Campbell. Automatic security assessment of critical cyber-infrastructures. In *Proceedings of the 38th Annual IEEE/IFIP International Conference on Dependable Systems and Networks (DSN)*, July 2008.
9. Davide Balzarotti, Mattia Monga, and Sabrina Sicari. Assessing the risk of using vulnerable components. In *Proceedings of the 2nd ACM workshop on Quality of Protection*, 2005.
10. Elizabeth Chew, Marianne Swanson, Kevin Stine, Nadya Bartol, Anthony Brown, and Will Robinson. *Performance Measurement Guide for Information Security*. National Institute of Standards and Technology, July 2008. NIST Special Publication 800-55 Revision 1.
11. F. Cuppens and R. Ortalo. Lambda: A language to model a database for detection of attacks. In *Proceedings of the Workshop on Recent Advances in Intrusion Detection*, 2000.
12. J. Dawkins and J. Hale. A systematic approach to multi-stage network attack analysis. In *Proceedings of Second IEEE International Information Assurance Workshop*, pages 48 – 56, April 2004.
13. Rinku Dewri, Nayot Poolsappasit, Indrajit Ray, and Darrell Whitley. Optimal security hardening using multi-objective optimization on attack tree models of networks. In *14th ACM Conference on Computer and Communications Security (CCS)*, 2007.
14. Marcel Frigault and Lingyu Wang. Measuring network security using Bayesian network-based attack graphs. In *Proceedings of the 3rd IEEE International Workshop on Security, Trust, and Privacy for Software Applications (STPSA'08)*, 2008.
15. Marcel Frigault, Lingyu Wang, Anoop Singhal, and Sushil Jajodia. Measuring network security using dynamic Bayesian network. In *Proceedings of the 4th ACM workshop on Quality of Protection*, 2008.
16. John Homer and Xinming Ou. SAT-solving approaches to context-aware enterprise network security management. *IEEE JSAC Special Issue on Network Infrastructure Configuration*, 27(3), April 2009.
17. John Homer, Xinming Ou, and David Schmidt. A sound and practical approach to quantifying security risk in enterprise networks. Technical report, Kansas State University, 2009.
18. Kyle Ingols, Matthew Chu, Richard Lippmann, Seth Webster, and Stephen Boyer. Modeling modern network attacks and countermeasures using attack graphs. In *25th Annual Computer Security Applications Conference (ACSAC)*, 2009.
19. Kyle Ingols, Richard Lippmann, and Keith Piwowarski. Practical attack graph generation for network defense. In *22nd Annual Computer Security Applications Conference (ACSAC)*, Miami Beach, Florida, December 2006.
20. Sushil Jajodia, Steven Noel, and Brian O'Berry. Topological analysis of network attack vulnerability. In V. Kumar, J. Srivastava, and A. Lazarevic, editors, *Managing Cyber Threats: Issues, Approaches and Challanges*, chapter 5. Kluwer Academic Publisher, 2003.
21. A. Jaquith. *Security Metrics: Replacing Fear, Uncertainty, and Doubt*. Addison Wesley, 2007.
22. Somesh Jha, Oleg Sheyner, and Jeannette M. Wing. Two formal analyses of attack graphs. In *Proceedings of the 15th IEEE Computer Security Foundations Workshop*, pages 49–63, Nova Scotia, Canada, June 2002.

23. Daniel Geer Jr., Kevin Soo Hoo, and Andrew Jaquith. Information security: Why the future belongs to the quants. *IEEE SECURITY & PRIVACY*, 2003.
24. Wei Li, Rayford B. Vaughn, and Yoginder S. Dandass. An approach to model network exploitations using exploitation graphs. *SIMULATION*, 82(8):523–541, 2006.
25. Richard Lippmann, Kyle Ingols, Chris Scott, Keith Piwowarski, Kendra Kratkiewicz, Mike Artz, and Robert Cunningham. Validating and restoring defense in depth using attack graphs. In *Military Communications Conference (MILCOM)*, Washington, DC, U.S.A., October 2006.
26. Richard Lippmann and Kyle W. Ingols. An annotated review of past papers on attack graphs. Technical report, MIT Lincoln Laboratory, March 2005.
27. Richard P. Lippmann, Kyle W. Ingols, Chris Scott, Keith Piwowarski, Kendra Kratkiewicz, Michael Artz, and Robert Cunningham. Evaluating and strengthening enterprise network security using attack graphs. Technical Report ESC-TR-2005-064, MIT Lincoln Laboratory, October 2005.
28. Pratyusa Manadhata, Jeannette Wing, Mark Flynn, and Miles McQueen. Measuring the attack surfaces of two FTP daemons. In *Proceedings of the 2nd ACM workshop on Quality of Protection*, 2006.
29. John McHugh. Quality of protection: measuring the unmeasurable? In *Proceedings of the 2nd ACM workshop on Quality of Protection (QoP)*, Alexandria, Virginia, USA, 2006.
30. John McHugh and James Tippett, editors. *Workshop on Information-Security-System Rating and Ranking (WISSRR)*. Applied Computer Security Associates, May 2001.
31. Peter Mell, Karen Scarfone, and Sasha Romanosky. *A Complete Guide to the Common Vulnerability Scoring System Version 2.0*. Forum of Incident Response and Security Teams (FIRST), June 2007.
32. National Institute of Standards and Technology. *Technology assessment: Methods for measuring the level of computer security*, 1985. NIST Special Publication 500-133.
33. S. Noel and J. Jajodia. Understanding complex network attack graphs through clustered adjacency matrices. In *Proceedings of the 21st Annual Computer Security Applications Conference*, 2005.
34. S. Noel and S. Jajodia. Proactive intrusion prevention and response via attack graphs. In Ryan Trost, editor, *Practical Intrusion Detection*. Addison-Wesley Professional, 2009.
35. Steven Noel and Sushil Jajodia. Managing attack graph complexity through visual hierarchical aggregation. In *VizSEC/DMSEC '04: Proceedings of the 2004 ACM workshop on Visualization and data mining for computer security*, pages 109–118, New York, NY, USA, 2004. ACM Press.
36. Steven Noel, Sushil Jajodia, Brian O'Berry, and Michael Jacobs. Efficient minimum-cost network hardening via exploit dependency graphs. In *19th Annual Computer Security Applications Conference (ACSAC)*, December 2003.
37. Xinming Ou. *A logic-programming approach to network security analysis*. PhD thesis, Princeton University, 2005.
38. Xinming Ou, Wayne F. Boyer, and Miles A. McQueen. A scalable approach to attack graph generation. In *13th ACM Conference on Computer and Communications Security (CCS)*, pages 336–345, 2006.
39. Xinming Ou, Sudhakar Govindavajhala, and Andrew W. Appel. MulVAL: A logic-based network security analyzer. In *14th USENIX Security Symposium*, 2005.
40. Joseph Pamula, Sushil Jajodia, Paul Ammann, and Vipin Swarup. A weakest-adversary security metric for network configuration security analysis. In *Proceedings of the 2nd ACM workshop on Quality of Protection*, 2006.
41. Cynthia Phillips and Laura Painton Swiler. A graph-based system for network-vulnerability analysis. In *NSPW '98: Proceedings of the 1998 workshop on New security paradigms*, pages 71–79. ACM Press, 1998.
42. Prasad Rao, Konstantinos F. Sagonas, Terrance Swift, David S. Warren, and Juliana Freire. XSB: A system for efficiently computing well-founded semantics. In *Proceedings of the 4th International Conference on Logic Programming and Non-Monotonic Reasoning (LP-NMR'97)*, pages 2–17, Dagstuhl, Germany, July 1997. Springer Verlag.

43. R. Ritchey and P. Ammann. Using model checking to analyze network vulnerabilities. In *Proceedings of the IEEE Symposium on Security and Privacy*, 2000.
44. Diptikalyan Saha. Extending logical attack graphs for efficient vulnerability analysis. In *Proceedings of the 15th ACM conference on Computer and Communications Security (CCS)*, 2008.
45. Mohamed Salim, Ehab Al-Shaer, and Latif Khan. A novel quantitative approach for measuring network security. In *INFOCOM 2008 Mini Conference*, 2008.
46. Oleg Sheyner. *Scenario Graphs and Attack Graphs*. PhD thesis, Carnegie Mellon, April 2004.
47. Oleg Sheyner, Joshua Haines, Somesh Jha, Richard Lippmann, and Jeannette M. Wing. Automated generation and analysis of attack graphs. In *Proceedings of the 2002 IEEE Symposium on Security and Privacy*, pages 254–265, 2002.
48. G. Stoneburner, C. Hayden, and A Feringa. Engineering principles for information technology security. Technical Report 800-27 (Rev A), National Institute of Standards and Technology, June 2004.
49. M. Swanson, N. Bartol, J. Sabato, J Hash, and L. Graffo. Security metrics guide for information technology systems. Technical Report 800-55, National Institute of Standards and Technology, July 2003.
50. Laura P. Swiler, Cynthia Phillips, David Ellis, and Stefan Chakerian. Computer-attack graph generation tool. In *DARPA Information Survivability Conference and Exposition (DISCEX II'01)*, volume 2, June 2001.
51. Steven J. Templeton and Karl Levitt. A requires/provides model for computer attacks. In *Proceedings of the 2000 workshop on New security paradigms*, pages 31–38. ACM Press, 2000.
52. T. Tidwell, R. Larson, K. Fitch, and J. Hale. Modeling Internet attacks. In *Proceedings of the 2001 IEEE Workshop on Information Assurance and Security*, West Point, NY, June 2001.
53. L. Wang, A. Singhal, and S. Jajodia. Measuring the overall security of network configurations using attack graphs. In *Proceedings of the 21st IFIP WG 11.3 Working Conference on Data and Applications Security*. Springer-Verlag, 2007.
54. Lingyu Wang, Tania Islam, Tao Long, Anoop Singhal, and Sushil Jajodia. An attack graph-based probabilistic security metric. In *Proceedings of The 22nd Annual IFIP WG 11.3 Working Conference on Data and Applications Security (DBSEC'08)*, 2008.
55. Lingyu Wang, Steven Noel, and Sushil Jajodia. Minimum-cost network hardening using attack graphs. *Computer Communications*, 29:3812–3824, November 2006.
56. Lingyu Wang, Anoop Singhal, and Sushil Jajodia. Measuring network security using attack graphs. In *Third Workshop on Quality of Protection (QoP)*, 2007.
57. Lingyu Wang, Anoop Singhal, and Sushil Jajodia. Measuring the overall security of network configurations using attack graphs. In *Proceedings of 21th IFIP WG 11.3 Working Conference on Data and Applications Security (DBSEC'07)*, 2007.
58. Anming Xie, Zhuhua Cai, Cong Tang, Jianbin Hu, and Zhong Chen. Evaluating network security with two-layer attack graphs. In *25th Annual Computer Security Applications Conference (ACSAC)*, 2009.